The purpose of this study guide is to provide supplemental educational material. It is not intended as a substitute or replacement of NEWS OF THE WORLD.

Published by SuperSummary, www.supersummary.com

ISBN – 9781087101217

For more information or to learn about our complete library of study guides, please visit http://www.supersummary.com

Please submit any comments, corrections, or questions to:
http://www.supersummary.com/support/

TABLE OF CONTENTS

Captain Jefferson Kyle Kidd
Johanna Leonberger
John Calley
Wilhelm and Anna Leonberger
Maria Luisa Betancort y Real
Elizabeth and Olympia
Britt Johnson
Simon Boudlin
Doris Dillon
Almay
The Horrell Brothers
The Merritt Brothers
Mrs. Gannet
Adolph

Paulette Jiles's novel, *News of the World*, tells the tale of 72-year-old Captain Jefferson Kyle Kidd and 10-year-old Johanna Leonberger's journey from Wichita, Texas to Castroville, Texas in 1870, and how that journey would forever and drastically change the course of each of their lives.

The story begins in Wichita, Texas, in the early spring of 1870, with Captain Kidd hanging posters advertising his reading of the news. He travels the state reading newspapers to people who live in remote areas and do not have access to the outside world. While in town he meets with an old acquaintance of his, Britt Johnson. Johnson has been hired by Johanna's aunt and uncle in southern Texas to transport her safely back to them, but because of the difficulty of the route, and the fact that Johanna is of European descent, and he and his companions are African American, he does not feel secure traveling with her through post-war Texas. Therefore, he asks Captain Kidd if he will take over the responsibility, which, with some reluctance, he accepts.

Captain Kidd and Johanna's journey is not an easy one. Post-war Texas is still recovering from the effects of the Civil War and especially from Reconstruction. Large tracts of the state are still frontier in nature and raids by bandits, and especially Indian tribes like the Kiowa and Comanche, are not uncommon. The Captain, however, is a man who is not unaccustomed to danger and warfare, having fought at the tender age of 16 during the War of 1812 (during which he also acquired the moniker, Captain, as he was later elected to that rank). The fact that Johanna does not speak English, and he knows only a few signs of Plains Indian Sign Language (and only a few words of Kiowa), make communication between the two difficult. Johanna, though of German descent, does not identify as white; rather, she is far more Kiowa than anything else.

Along the route to Castroville, a small town near San Antonio, where Johanna's relatives reside, the Captain does his best to earn much needed funds with his readings while also trying to teach Johanna English and prepare her for reintegration into white, European-American society. Many troubles lie for them along the road: dealing with Indians, men who wish to do harm to Johanna (which results in a gunfight and the display of Johanna's ingenuity in using dimes as shotgun pellets), the political turmoil of Texas, the natural elements, and the societal difficulties associated with Johanna's reintegration. For example, when Johanna bathes in a town's river naked and is chased around by a woman who wants to get her clothed and "proper," or when Johanna steals two chickens, unfamiliar with the idea of pets or property.

The Captain is a kind and long-suffering man who is sympathetic to Johanna's plight. Along the route, Johanna comes to see him as her guardian, even calling him *Kontah* (grandpa in Kiowa). The further they travel, the better her English becomes. They learn to work together; Johanna eventually joins the Captain during his readings and collects the dimes that everyone is supposed to pay as admission, being very skilled at making sure everyone pays. They grow fond of one another, which makes parting difficult.

As the story draws towards its end, and as the Captain and Johanna arrive in the small village of D'Hanis, near Castroville, the Captain meets a man along the route whom he engages to ask for directions. He also asks the man to announce Johanna's return to Wilhelm and Anna

Leonberger. The man, Adolph, is a fellow German and rushes to deliver the news, ecstatic to hear of her survival. Once they arrive, however, there is no emotion on Wilhelm's face, and he behaves as though Johanna's return is simply a business deal. The Captain remains for a while to see to Johanna's transition, and learns that the Leonbergers are not kind or even well-liked people. Adolph eventually tells him that he should not leave Johanna with them. This places him in a dilemma. His honor and moral code do not allow him to just take her away. He made a promise to return her, and accepted money to do so.

He leaves for his home in San Antonio, but he cannot forget Johanna. He even goes so far as investigating adoption laws. Even though the outlook is bleak for legal recourse, it only takes him one day in San Antonio before he makes his decision to return to D'Hanis in order to reason or bribe the Leonbergers into taking better care of Johanna. He leaves the next morning.

As he comes up to the Leonberger farmhouse, he espies Johanna in the distance, tending to some chores. He calls out to her. The Leonbergers have been beating her. He tells her to drop what she is doing and come with him. Johanna is very happy and more than willing to leave with him. The love that grew between them over their long journey is not a connection that can easily be broken.

The final chapter of the story summarizes the remainder of not only Johanna's and the Captain's lives, but also that of a few of the more important, secondary characters. Johanna becomes a proper southern belle through the Captain's love and kindness, though she will forever remain Kiowa at heart, a woman who enjoys the freedom of nature. She eventually marries a man whom she accompanies on cattle drives. The Captain lives a few more years and when he dies, his will states that he wants to be buried with his runner's medal that he received during the War of 1812, that "he had a message to deliver, contents unknown" (209).

Chapters 1-5

Chapter 1 Summary

It is February 1870, in Wichita Falls, Texas. Captain Jefferson Kyle Kidd (aka Captain Kidd, or simply the Captain), an older gentleman, rides into town. He tacks up his posters and changes into his "reading" clothes in the stable. He is there to read to the townsfolk the news from various newspapers at a charge of 10¢ per person. He used to own and run his own printing press, but lost his business because of the Civil War. Now he travels from town to town keeping people informed of the "news of the world" (1).

He reads an article from the *Boston Morning Journal* about the passing of the 15th Amendment, which allows all men the right to vote regardless of color, explaining to the people, without any mincing of words, that that means black men are allowed to vote. From the *New York Tribune* he reads to them about the ship, Hansa, sinking from pack ice in the North Pole near Greenland. From the *Philadelphia Inquirer*, he tells them about the renowned British physicist, James Maxwell, and his work in electromagnetism, which he uses in order to bore the audience and prime them to be ready to leave, knowing that the majority of the audience are not interested in matters of scientific discovery, and are not educated enough to understand the import thereof.

He notices a man in the back whom, he recognizes as Britt Johnson. Britt Johnson is a free black man who works in hauling freight from town to town. He wants to talk to Captain Kidd.

6

Outside, Britt shows him a young, white girl in his wagon who is dressed in Native American garb. Britt explains that the girl, Johanna Leonberger, was captured by the Kiowa when she was only 4 years old from Castroville, a small town near San Antonio, Texas, but that they traded her to an agent for various supplies. The army had threatened the Kiowa and other tribes with violence if they didn't turn over all captives. Furthermore, he was paid a $50 gold coin by the girl's aunt and uncle, Wilhelm and Anna Leonberger, for her safe return to San Antonio. However, on economic grounds (he didn't have any goods to buy and sell in San Antonio), and because of the simple fact that a group of black men transporting a white girl over so long a distance would not look good, and would be dangerous for them, Britt wants the Captain to take over the responsibility of delivering Johanna to her aunt and uncle. The Captain tries to argue against his ability to, but Britt always has a counter argument. He then explains how he hadn't thought about him (the Captain) until he'd seen his posters and knew he was in town. He says it's destiny that he should be there when he was needing to pass the girl on to someone else. The Captain reluctantly agrees to take Johanna. Britt gives him the gold coin.

Before leaving, Britt warns him about how children who have spent time among the Indians change, that they are never the same as they once were. He relates how his own son was kidnapped by the Kiowa before he had taken him back and how he had changed, how he no longer likes roofs, has problems learning to write, and is fearful. He tells the Captain to be careful.

Johanna slides down in the back of Britt's wagon, where she has been sitting stiff and erect like a statue the entire time, and covers herself with a blanket. She will spend the night there.

Chapter 2 Summary

Johanna receives clothing from the women of Wichita Falls. However, she either does not care for the new clothes or doesn't know how to wear them properly because she allows the hem of her dress to drag in the red mud, not holding it up when she walks.

The Captain goes off and purchases a wagon with the coin Britt gave him. It's a used wagon with the words "Curative Waters East Mineral Springs Texas" (14) painted across the side, but it has a spring bench seat that will be comfortable on the bumpy, rocky roads. It's possible to spread a canvas tarp over the wagon in case of bad weather. The Captain plans on having his pack horse pull the wagon, while the other one walks behind in tow. The Captain changes from his clothes into attire better suited for the road, carefully packing his reading clothes in a carpet bag and his nice hat in a tin box. He then goes off in search of Britt one last time.

The Captain finds Britt finishing loading his wagon. He sees his boy whom he remarks is a hard-worker but who also seems to constantly look at his father anxiously. He asks Britt about the best roads to take. Britt recommends the road along the Red River towards Spanish Fort, then from there to Dallas, and then the Miridian road south towards San Antonio. Britt asks to see the gun the Captain carries. He pulls it out from behind him and gives it to Britt. Britt says how that it's a gun he would have had when he was 10, and then gives the Captain his own Smith and Wesson, stating how he is very grateful for the Captain's help. They then say goodbye to one another.

The Captain climbs up into his wagon with Johanna, who we learn is 10 years old. There is a pale-haired man and two other men with him watching the Captain and Johanna from the shadows, the same man the Captain recognized in Chapter 1 as someone of a "not commendable reputation" (4). They continue to watch as the Captain and Johanna leave town.

Chapter 3 Summary

The chapter opens with a flashback to the Captain's past. It's some time during the War of 1812, and he is 16, serving in the Georgia militia as a private. He has fought in the Battle of Horseshoe Bend under Andrew Jackson. His Captain was a man named Thompson. During the battle, his unit was under heavy fire. Thompson was out beyond the barricades and Captain Kidd went out to save him. He was able to bring him back to safety, but Thompson had already sustained mortal wounds. Captain Kidd was himself wounded in the thigh. After the battle, Kidd was promoted to the rank of sergeant, and he studiously asked others about the requirements and duties of a sergeant, believing that "written information was what mattered in this world" (22), even though he was often made fun of because of it.

The Captain was soon given the responsibility of transporting prisoners, which he hated, to Pensacola, Florida. There he learned the ways of interrogation, hand-to-hand combat (wrestling), and other military skills. Within a few months, he became a messenger, a runner carrying information between units. This was a job he loved doing. He was built for it. He was long-haired, over 6 feet tall, with runner's muscles. Being raised in the mountainous terrain of Georgia tempered him for the endeavors of being a runner for the Provost Marshall. These are his best memories during this time period, and he recalls how he enjoyed the solitude of the work and the amazement of the feeling of being "granted the life and the task for which one is meant" (24).

After the war, he returned to Georgia and became an apprentice in a printing press in Macon, GA. Following his mother's death, and learning of the events of the Alamo, he left for Texas. In San Antonio, he opened up his own printing press. He learned Spanish so that he could print things in both languages. He met his wife there, a younger girl of Spanish descent. He remembers his wife fondly, but there is something painful in their history that isn't yet mentioned. Her name was Maria Luisa Betancort y Real. They had two girls together.

Later on, during the Mexican-American War, he was called back into military service even though he was 50 years old. He was promoted to the rank of captain, and from then on he was known as Captain Kidd. It was his job to organize communications between President Taylor's forces and the Texas Rangers. He recalls a time in February of 1847, while with a young unit of a Texas Rangers in the hills above Monterrey, in Mexico, when he shared some of his previous war experiences with the troops. They were looking for some wisdom from the veteran. He told them to take care of one another, because you never know who will get shot.

During the night, sitting alone in front of the fire, the Captain had reflected on the news he was charged to dispatch. This news was in regard to the infighting and splintered command structure of the Mexican army, and how that "if people had true knowledge of the world perhaps they would not take up arms and so perhaps he could be an aggregator of information from distant places and then the world would be a more peaceful place" (29). It was an illusion that lasted until he was 65. However, he later came to believe that what people really needed was not only information but also stories from remote and exotic places, so that they could forget about their own troubles for a while.

Chapter 4 Summary

Johanna is walking alongside the wagon, barefoot, singing a tune in the Kiowa language. She feels very alone. She sings to keep from crying. The Captain is driving the wagon. She considers options like running away or starving herself to death. It's drizzling out. The Captain senses her anxiety and takes the time to show her his armaments in an attempt to console her. At first, she seems bewildered, but she makes a quick sharp nod that the Captain takes as a sign of understanding, though he doubts that she believes that the two of them are on the same team.

They continue on. He remarks how different she is, that she carries herself like a Native Americans though she is blonde-haired and blue-eyed with freckles on her cheeks. He remarks how white people are more open, unguarded. The Indians, on the other hand, have a sort of "kinetic stillness" (33). He then attempts to teach Johanna her name by pointing at her, which is something that startles and worries her because the Kiowa never point at others unless they mean to do harm. She wonders if he's trying to use evil magic against her. However, he continues to point at her nonchalantly, repeating her name, enunciating clearly with emphasis on the syllables. He then points to himself and does the same for his name, Captain. He does this until she repeats what he tells her and he gets the idea she understands.

They come to a river crossing. It isn't easy, but they cross without too much difficulty, even though one of the wheels

cracks and will need to be repaired once they reach Spanish
Fort. They stop for the night, and the Captain again
attempts to teach her some English and communicate with
her. He shows her the stove he brought along and how it
works. Johanna is quizzical. She is surprised by the heat
and fire of the stove and makes the Kiowa sign for fire,
which the Captain recognizes. He understands some of the
sign-language of the Plains Indians and signs "Yes" to her.
He then makes a dinner of coffee, cornbread, and bacon.
He gives Johanna her portion. She doesn't eat it straight
away. Rather she sits awhile with it, then sings over it,
before finally eating. After the meal, he sits and leans back
against his saddle. She lies on a blanket, never taking her
eyes off of him. He reads the *Chicago Tribune* and tells her
about a meat-processing plant in Chicago. The Captain
thinks about his role as a man striving towards the
condition of humanity to protect children, to kill for them if
necessary. He shares his opinion with her about the
importance of the written word.

Before going to sleep he prays for Britt, who is often in
harm's way, for his daughters, his son-in-law, and his
grandsons who are all going to make their way from
Georgia to him in Texas. He also prays for himself and
Johanna.

Chapter 5 Summary

The duo approach the town of Spanish Fort. The horses
grow restless and they hear riders in the distance. It's a US
Cavalry patrol. The Captain makes a sign to Johanna to let
her know that they are friends. Nevertheless, Johanna is
frightened and cowers in the back of the wagon. He
recognizes that she is afraid he is going to hand her over to
the soldiers. The cavalry men draw close, led by a
lieutenant (LT) who speaks to the Captain. The LT is

friendly and asks simple questions, especially about Johanna. The Captain explains the situation and shows the LT the papers from the Agent. The LT questions the Captain about what weapons he is carrying. The Captain only admits to the shotgun (Johanna is in the back underneath some blankets, hiding with the revolver). The Captain is slightly disrespectful at this point, interjecting his dislike of the law that prevents people from carrying revolvers in post-war Texas. The LT doesn't take offense, even commiserating with the Captain.

Because he does not turn her over to the soldiers, Johanna becomes much friendlier and happier with the Captain, even deciding to ride on the bench in the wagon with him, something she has refused to do previously.

They make their way into Spanish Fort, also known as Red River Station, which is a crossroads town full of people making their way to other destinations. The chaos and noise is unsettling for the Captain and he wonders, if it is so bad for him, then how bad must it be for Johanna. The Captain begins readying the wagon for the evening, and removes the revolver shells from their hiding place in the flour, moving them to a spot under the bench of the wagon. Johanna's English is slowly improving, and he asks her to ready the stove. She tells him "Yes" and moves off to gather wood.

There has been flooding that has made further crossing difficult. There are many people waiting in and around the town for it to subside, so that they can move on.

Chapters 1-5 Analysis

The first five chapters establish the personalities and characteristics of the two main protagonists, Captain Kidd and Johanna Leonberger. The reader quickly learns how patient and sympathetic the Captain is with Johanna, and how she learns to trust him.

These chapters also establish the setting and plot—post-war Texas, 1870, and the journey from Wichita Falls to San Antonio. Furthermore, it introduces many of the difficulties the two will face: the difficulty of returned captives to reintegrate, meaning that traveling with Johanna won't be like it would with a normal girl. The danger of Indian raiding parties is mentioned, and the danger of being lightly armed due to Reconstruction laws. These chapters also establish a character who will turn out to be the main antagonist and biggest problem the Captain and Johanna will have to face; this character is Almay, the man mentioned early on in the novel. The reader, at this juncture, is not aware of the problems Almay will pose.

Many of the symbols and motifs of the novel are also introduced in these first chapters, such the "curative waters" wagon, which runs in the background as Johanna and the Captain are slowly "healed" by one another; the jorongo; and the need for protection and security.

There is an unconventional aspect to the text itself in that it does not follow traditional punctuation rules. There is a complete lack of quotation marks for the dialogue of the characters. The reasons for doing this are not anything specific; however, what it does do for this text is to blend the narration and dialogue together so that the demarcation between the two doesn't exist. It's as though whoever is narrating the story is also narrating the dialogue.

The language—that is, the vocabulary and syntax—is also rather simple and straightforward. There is nothing experimental in style. Aside from the lack of quotation marks, another aspect of punctuation is tooled with within the text: commas are used very sparingly. This forces sentences to be read without pauses, creating a fluidity in the reading that simulates actual speech, much like a news report.

Chapters 6-10

Chapter 6 Summary

The Captain leaves Johanna with the task of the stove and goes off to speak to the man who takes care of the Masonic Lodge, so he can rent it for his reading. He bemoans the fact that with Johanna he is unable to stay in a hotel and eat in a restaurant because he does not trust that she can behave herself under such circumstances. He then hangs up his advertisements for the reading around town.

The Captain notices a man sitting at the window of a store whom he knows: Simon Boudlin, a fiddler. He walks into the store and chats with Simon. The Captain tells him about renting the lodge, and Simon tells him about how he just finished playing for the Dancing School because the guitarist they'd previously hired to play busted all his strings tuning his guitar too high. The Captain tells Simon about Johanna. Simon had heard of someone else named Kiowa Dutch who'd also been abducted by the Kiowa when he was younger and how odd he was—how he was never the same as before. The Captain then asks him if he and his female friend, Doris, wouldn't mind watching over Johanna while he reads because he is worried she will run away if left unsupervised.

The Captain, Doris, and Simon find Johanna in the wagon. She has made dinner. Doris presents her with a doll that Johanna mistakes for an idol. She says things to it in

Kiowa. Doris feels sympathy and sadness for Johanna, seeing her as an unfinished child who has already experienced two creations. The Captain asks Doris how she came to this knowledge. Doris replies in Gaelic, *an Gorta Mór*, the Great Hunger, aka the Irish Famine. Johanna reminds Doris of her dead sister. She wants the Captain to leave Johanna with them, permanently, saying that she and Simon will care for her. The Captain tells her that he has to take her to her people in San Antonio because he was paid to do so.

He ruminates about the situation Johanna is in, how she is a cause of trouble to those around her, and how she is not truly wanted by anyone.

Johanna retreats to the corner of the wagon and the protection of her large Mexican poncho.

Chapter 7 Summary

The Captain reads of various news from around the world to a crowd of people who have gathered inside the Masonic Lodge to listen. He begins by reading to them from *The London Daily News* about the Franco-Prussian War. The audience is amazed not by the war but by the fact that they are hearing about it from a paper from England, amazed at hearing about news from so far away. The Captain is dressed in his reading outfit, which presents him as someone wise and authoritative. He reads them a story form the *Philadelphia Inquirer* about Dr. Schliemann searching for the ancient city of Troy, and about telegraph wires laid between Britain and India. He thinks he sees the pale-headed man again.

After he is finished reading, Simon enters and informs him that Johanna is gone.

Outside, the weather has grown worse. There is a rainstorm raging at full strength. The Red River is very flooded, but nevertheless, Simon and the Captain go off in search of Johanna. For the first time, the Captain openly complains about his task, and about the inconvenience of looking after Johanna. He and Simon find her atop a large stone trying to get the attention of a group of Kiowa on the other bank of the river. She shouts to them in Kiowa, but they cannot hear or understand her over the din of the raging river. The Captain notices the Kiowa are carrying Sharps rifles. One of the Indians fires a warning shot, informing her, the Captain, and Simon that they shouldn't come any closer. The Captain runs up, grabs Johanna, and pulls her off the rock and runs. They hear another rifle report and a .50 caliber bullet rips into a tree.

Back in the wagon, the Captain is alone with Johanna, who is sleeping. He bemoans the situation, but resolves, nevertheless, to see the job through because he promised he would. He reflects on the fact that she has not yet cried, not once, in spite of all she has been through.

They leave Spanish Fort, but the Captain has forgotten to change to wheel, which means he will have to do it in Dallas. He hopes it will hold out until then.

After paying for the lodge and purchasing necessary supplies, he doesn't have a lot of money left over. Johanna sings to herself often. She accepts her situation with marked resilience. The Captain tries to talk to her again. He talks to her about her aunt and uncle and remembers that they are Germans. He uses the German words for aunt and uncle (*tante* and *onkel*), which she comprehends. She opens and closes her hands, evoking a memory, and says, in German, that her mother and father are dead.

The pair arrive in Dallas and Johanna is even more intimidated by the town than she was of Spanish Fort. The Captain, on the other hand, is glad, this time, to be in civilization. He heads towards a livery stable to get the wagon repaired and knows the owner, a widow named Mrs. Gannet. There, he changes clothes. Mrs. Gannet tells him she will send out his travel clothes to be cleaned and agrees to keep an eye on Johanna while he goes off to buy some newspapers and find a hotel room.

Johanna remains cloaked in her poncho and reaches out a hand towards the Captain, fearing he will leave her. He touches her on the forehead and does his best to reassure here. He wants to tell her he will be back in an hour, but knows that she will not understand. Before he leaves, he tells her to "sit. Stay" (70).

Chapter 8 Summary

The Captain heads off to rent two rooms at a hotel and then takes a bath, which costs him 50. Afterwards, he finds the proprietor of the Broadway Playhouse and engages the small theater for the night, for his readings. He then goes to the local printing press, Thurber's News and Printing Establishment. He knows Thurber personally and is jealous of the man's business. Thurber asks the Captain about his travels and wants to know if it isn't getting burdensome for him to be doing what he's doing. The Captain answers grumpily that he isn't that old yet, and takes offense. Nevertheless, he buys copies of the *Philadelphia Enquirer, Chicago Tribune, London Times, New York Herald,* and a Spanish-language, Mexican paper, *El Clarion.* He also has advertisements for his readings printed.

After leaving the printing office, the Captain walks around town tacking up his notices, all the while contemplating his situation with Johanna. He is grumpier and more negative than before, lamenting that he has already raised two daughters. His conscience, however, which sounds to him much like the voice of his father, continues to hold him to his promise.

On his way back to Johanna and Mrs. Gannet, the Captain picks up some dinner: barbecued meat, bread, and squash. Johanna is clearly happy to see him return. He teaches her the word "dinner." They sit down to eat, and Johanna uses the knife to cut off a large hunk of meat. She tosses it between her hands until it's cool enough to bite into. Barbecue sauce drips down her wrists. The Captain attempts to teach her to use a fork. She tries, but can't quite get the hang of it, and eventually tosses the fork away in frustration. The Captain sympathizes with her: she has lost her parents, was raised by the Kiowa, sold for blankets, transferred from stranger to stranger, culture to culture, and now even has to learn to eat with utensils that don't make sense to her.

At some point later on, the Captain informs Johanna that she will need to stay in a hotel room and try to not break the windows while he prepares his reading. He takes her greasy hand in his and they walk off together.

Chapter 9 Summary

The Captain locks the hotel room door behind him and hears Johanna begin a Kiowa chant. He remarks how he has no idea how to understand her chanting, whether she has reconciled herself to the room, will hang herself, set fire to the room, or just simply go to sleep.

Downstairs, he has a brief conversation with the desk clerk, who is bothered by Johanna's chanting and cannot commiserate with her at all, wondering why she isn't wonderfully happy to be away from the Kiowa. He implores the Captain to go and get Mrs. Gannet, because he can't listen to her chant all night.

The Captain finds Mrs. Gannet with her hair in complex and attractive braids, giving orders to her drunken stableman. The Captain asks her if she wouldn't mind spending the night with Johanna in her room. He would even pay her a dollar to do it. She smiles at him and says that she would be delighted to help. For the first time in weeks, he dares to hope that in the evening he will not feel worried, won't have to fear Johanna running off and getting hurt.

Mrs. Gannet has prepared some divinity fudge for Johanna and offers her a piece. Johanna signs to the Captain the Kiowa sign for poison. He asks Mrs. Gannet to take a bite first. She understands, takes a bite of the fudge to show Johanna it's safe, and then offers her the other half. She accepts it and eats it, but doesn't seem to know what to think of it. The Captain leaves their room to go to his.

He begins writing a letter to his daughters. From his letter, we learn his daughters' names, Elizabeth and Olympia. Elizabeth's husband lost his right arm in the war, and Olympia's husband was killed. The Captain wants them all to travel to live with him in Texas, citing many positive aspects of the state, mentioning several advantages and hiding or simply not mentioning anything negative, and also not addressing the many dangers that the road entails. He writes to them about some property that once belonged to their mother's family, the Betancorts, and asks his daughter, Elizabeth, to write to a certain Señor Amistad de Lara to inquire about specifics. While he is writing the letter, Johanna is in the other room, banging against the wall and calling out his name. He bangs back from time to time, says her name, and tells her to go to sleep. He listens as Mrs. Gannet sings to Johanna. He wonders why he hasn't shown Mrs. Gannet more attention, and then remembers it's because his daughters wouldn't take it well, and would feel he was being disloyal to the memory of their mother.

We learn that the Captain is 71 years old.

Eventually, Johanna falls asleep, or at least the noise has died down. It is nearly 8pm, time for him to go and do his readings.

Chapter 10 Summary

Inside the playhouse, before the readings, the Captain ruminates on the state of Texas politics: that the state is still under Marshall Law, that there is strong political infighting within the Republican Party, that the gubernatorial race is heated, and that the current political situation will make clearing up the title to the Betancort lands a lengthy process.

He greets the crowd the way he normally does: by thanking the host and commenting on the roads he's travelled getting there. He begins with a story from a foreign paper, this time from the *London Times*. He tells the crowd about how the British Colonial government wants to conduct a census of all the peoples under their rule and how the Hindu tribes rebelled. The crowd agrees in unspoken unison on the inability for rational thought in those types of people. He reads to them about the packing plants in Chicago, sparking future business ideas in many. He reads them several more stories, anything and everything so long as it doesn't have anything to do with state politics.

At the end of the reading, a man from the crowd questions the Captain as to why he isn't reading from Governor Davis's state journal, to which the Captain replies it is because, if he did so, there would be an open brawl within minutes, perhaps even shooting, elaborating that no one can talk about Texas politics calmly and rationally anymore. He cites the two US soldiers in the back standing guard.

As he is leaving the theater, the pale-haired man from earlier accosts him. We learn his name is Almay, and he wants to buy Johanna from him. It isn't directly stated, but the Captain understands that Almay wants her for purposes in prostitution. The Captain reflects how it's a good thing he doesn't have his revolver with him; otherwise, he would be very tempted to shoot Almay right then and there. Almay even lightly threatens him, stating that he is being a reasonable business man and wanting to avoid problems, even though he could take the girl from him with force out on the road. The Captain is wise, as Almay is escorted by two Caddos Indians, his hired goons, and avoids a direct refusal, rather offering to meet him tomorrow morning at 7am, to discuss a price.

The Captain then rushes to the stables and gets the wagon and horses ready to leave, giving instructions to the drunken stableman. He hurries over to the hotel and informs Mrs. Gannet that they have to leave tonight. He takes leave of Mrs. Gannet, asking her for the honor of calling upon her on his return to Dallas (a fancy, round-about-way of asking someone out back then).

He and Johanna take the road south, knowing that Almay and his Caddos expect him to take the Meridian Road southwest. He plans on going west later in the night to connect to the Meridian Road, all in an attempt to delay the others from catching up to them. He mentally takes inventory of his armaments and knows they are lacking for a full-out fight. The country south of Dallas is sparsely populated and Indian raids are to be expected.

In the night, they see lights burning in the windows of a farm house. Johanna cries out, "sau-podle" (98), portending death. The Captain tells Johann to ignore it, to imagine it was just a night hawk they'd seen.

Chapters 6-10 Analysis

The difficulties of returned captive children are reinforced with the tale of Kiowa Dutch. In fact, the major theme of these five chapters is to illustrate in further depth the issues and problems facing Johanna as the Captain guides her back into white-American society.

Chapter 7 is an important turning point for Johanna as she attempts to rejoin the Kiowa, her last attempt to return to the life she'd previously known. They will not take her, and don't even recognize her, nor understand that she's speaking to them in their own language. This scene symbolizes her disconnect with the Kiowa world—that even though she wishes to return, she never will. There is no road leading back for her.

Johanna is, for a person solely accustomed to life on the plains, intimidated by the loud noises and tall buildings of an American town. The small junction of Red River is bad enough, but Dallas is even worse for her. Her unfamiliarity with common, Anglo things like fudge, and her innate distrust of strangers, is further shown in her interactions with Mrs. Gannet. The *jorongo* gains stronger significance for her as a symbol of safety and protection: it's literally her security blanket.

Chapter 9 reinforces the warning that Britt gave the Captain in the first chapter, when he told him that his own son felt insecure indoors. Johanna's first night in a hotel room is fraught with difficulties for her, shown by her chanting and banging on the walls for the Captain, and with her inability to sleep. Though it's never addressed in the book, it isn't dissimilar to a person's first time camping under the stars, the main difference being that the returned captive seems to never fully adjust to life under a roof.

As much as these chapters illustrate Johanna's problems, they also display the Captain's great patience with and sympathy for Johanna. Though he begins to feel the burden of the responsibility of caring for her, he never once takes it out on her, as doing so would go beyond his code of honor. It is a much deeper characteristic of his that allows him to deeply sympathize with her, even bordering on empathy. The reader gets an even better sense of just how important these two characters are becoming for one another.

It's also interesting to note, though it is never further developed in the novel, that integration into American society is something experienced by many groups. This is first illustrated with the character of Doris, and her brief tale of coming over during the Irish Potato Famine and the loss of her sister. Doris finds certain similarities between her experience and that of Johanna's, which makes her want to reach out and care for her. Through Doris, the reader gains another perspective, one that is, for most Americans, more accessible, as the woes of Irish immigrants is better known than those of white children captured by Native Americans and then returned.

A further theme solidly established in these chapters, and subsequently reinforced throughout the novel, is the juxtaposition of differing cultures: European-American society and the cultures of the Plains Indians, specifically the Kiowa. The two cultures are neutrally juxtaposed, neither culture being portrayed as superior to the other, just different.

Chapters 11-13

Chapter 11 Summary

By morning, Johanna and the Captain are about one mile from the Brazos River. The Captain recognizes the area; it's known as Carlyle Springs. He notices a path that leads up to a ravine that looks down over the river and decided it's a good place to make camp.

He maneuvers the wagon uphill, searching for a good place for some cover. Atop a ravine, he finds a flat area covered in sumac and stumps, providing concealment, and a rocky embrasure for cover. He hands Johanna some bacon and she tells him she will cook. Her English is better than before.

As she is cooking, the Captain notices smoke off in the distance. Then, all of a sudden, the stove, whereat Johanna is cooking, erupts from a fired rifle round. The Captain takes cover among the rocks and Johanna underneath the cart. Rounds pop around them from time to time. The Captain remains calm and cool-witted, thinking out the situation and how best to deal with the attackers. He remarks how it isn't the first time someone has wanted to kill him, but the first time he has been so outnumbered and outgunned. He recognizes the report of their rifles as that of larger, Henry rifles. He is a bit surprised that Almay and his Caddos goons have decided to kill him so quickly. He had expected them to at least try and barter with him one more time. Johanna is under the wagon. She braids her hair, and doesn't seem surprised or astonished at all by anything that is happening.

Because he is low on ammunition, he waits for them to draw closer to him before he begins returning fire. He notices that all three of them are coming up the path he'd taken earlier, single file, and infers that they are over-confident.

The Captain wonders just how heavily armed they are, and as they get closer, he can confirm that they have two rifles, while the third has a handgun. They attempt to attack from the right and left and outflank him. He shoots the rifle out of one of their hands and then wounds the Caddo as he goes back to pick up the rifle. Johanna herself goes on the offensive. She ties up her dress so that it looks like she is wearing baggy Turkish pants, takes the large iron lid-lifter, and begins loosing a large stone. The Captain is amazed at her bravery, realizing that this, too, is not her first gunfight. She looses the stone, sending it crashing down towards the other two men. They run and the Captain fires, but he misses on every shot, which causes him to be furious with himself. The man the Captain was firing at disappears from view.

Chapter 12 Summary

The Captain and Johanna are still in the middle of their gunfight with Almay and the two Caddos. He is running low on ammunition. He is proud of Johanna and her quick thinking.

A round comes in at them, splintering the rock in front of the Captain and causing a piece to chip off and strike him in the forehead, just above his right eye. The wound bleeds. He tells himself how much he cannot get wounded, killed, how he cannot fail for Johanna's sake, how he needs to save her. He even goes so far to think, "some people were born unsupplied with a human conscience, and those people needed killing" (110). Johanna hands him their canteen. He takes a sip and realizes that, in a siege, not only do they not have enough ammunition but also not enough water to last very long.

He spots a rifle barrel downrange, aims carefully, and fires. He hears a cry of pain. However, he now only has fourteen rounds left. He tries to get Johanna to leave on Pasha, his stronger and faster horse, but she will not leave his side. He begins to feel the desperation of the situation, and fires off five more rounds that he wishes he had saved because they were not good opportunities.

Johanna crawls back over to him with the shotgun and the bag of dimes. He tries to explain the ineffectiveness of the light birdshot, the only ammunition he has for the shotgun, and also that the money is useless, because Almay will not be bought off. It turns out, however, that Johanna didn't have any of those things in mind. She wants him to use the dimes as projectiles for the shotgun. He is amazed by her ingenuity, and thinks that her idea just might work. They begin loading shells with dimes. However, to make this work, they will also need to play a small game of deception. He fires off a few rounds of the birdshot to make Almay believe that the birdshot is all he has left. It appears to work, as Almay laughs and teases him. Almay calls out he wants to make a deal still, that he can be reasonable. The Captain doesn't believe him for a second and judges Almay's intentions to be that of a ruse, that Almay just wants to delay him long enough for the two Caddos to get into a better position. The Captain uses his own form of deception, goading Almay out from behind his rock and getting him to move within range of the new, super-charged dimeshot. It works, and he unloads a round into the head of Almay, who falls over dead. The two Caddos, seeing their boss shot and killed, run off with no more desire to fight. For good measure, the Captain lets off another round into the backside of one of the Caddos.

He is overjoyed that they were able to pull off their plan, that everything worked out. Johanna is excited and happy, too, and begins chanting the victory song of the Kiowa. She holds a knife above her head, and moves off down the ravine towards Almay's body, to scalp him. The Captain goes after her, in order to stop her, telling her that in no way whatsoever is she going to scalp him. He tells her "it is considered very impolite" (118).

Chapter 13 Summary

The Captain and Johanna have some difficulty driving the wagon back down the ravine. The Captain's nerves are still humming. Johanna sits in the back of the wagon, holding the revolver. The Captain has unloaded it, but it comforts her nevertheless to have it in her hands. Once they make it back down, the Captain needs a rest. He is exhausted. He muses over Almay, how his child prostitution ring has come to an end. They stop for the night for some much-needed rest. The Captain wonders how it is that he isn't haunted by war memories, that he can fall asleep peacefully and sleep like the dead.

In the morning, Johanna wakes him up with breakfast. After the meal, he takes his time recovering. He still feels the effects of the fight. The wound above his right eye is swollen, but not badly. Johanna is playing in the creek, singing, and splashing. Even though he hasn't fully recuperated, they move on.

They arrive at the Brazos ferry landing, but they don't see a ferry, which means that, once again, they have to make a river crossing on their own. Fortunately, this one goes off easier than the first. While they travel, the Captain contemplates Johanna's fate. She is happy while they travel, and he thinks back on examples of other captives he has known or heard of who were eventually returned to their families. He remembers that two of them had starved themselves to death. Others became alcoholics or simply outsiders. All of them had difficulties re-acclimating to the civilized world. For the first time, he begins to doubt the goal of his mission.

Johanna likes to play language games along the route. She enjoys learning new words and creating new sentences, especially ones that don't make much sense: for example, *the horse shoots the gun*. The Captain humors her as best he can, but it quickly gets on his nerves. At one point, he tells her to shut up, which she just parrots back to him.

She does fall absolutely silent, though, as a group of men on horseback approach them. She crawls down, making herself as small as possible. The Captain is wary of their intentions. The leader of the men, a man with a black beard, questions the Captain about the shot-up wagon and about the girl. The Captains tells them about his taking her back to her relatives. The group has heard about children being captured by Indians, but has never actually known one personally. The black-bearded man gives Johanna a piece of saltwater taffy. He then asks the Captain about his political standing. The Captain realizes reading the news in Durand will be problematic, but he is so short of funds that he doesn't have much of a choice. One of the other men tells him that no one who supports Davis is allowed into Erath County. The men are very anti-Davis, whom they blame for the anarchy in their town. The Captain realizes that what they really want is a bribe. He asks the black-bearded man directly how much it will cost to let them pass. After a short pause, he asks for 50¢.

Chapters 11-13 Analysis

These three chapters contain the traditional, quintessential "gunfight scene" found in so many a western story. It's the showdown between the novel's hero, Captain Kidd, and the novel's most villain, Almay, the child-prostitute pimp. Aside from being the novel's greatest action scene, it further develops Johanna's character and illustrates the Captain's martial abilities, abilities he has developed over a long life and his war experiences. Furthermore, it provides food for thought about life among the Plains Indians. How much war (this is the period known as The Indian Wars), do the Native American tribes see that a girl of only 10 has already experienced war/violence/a gun fight ? Johanna does not at all behave like a typical child. She is calm under fire, brave to the point of recklessness, and, even more astonishingly, she is able to keep a cool head and be creative: she exposes herself to fire while prying a boulder loose, sending it crashing down upon her enemies; furthermore, she has the ingenious idea to use the dimes as buckshot for the shotgun, the thing that ultimately saves them both.

This scene is also the turning point in the Captain's and Johanna's relationship. Just like soldiers who have fought together, the Captain and Johanna are now bound to one another through the shared experience of mutual combat— brothers-in-arms, so to speak. From here on out, the question of whether or not they will actually be able to part from one another is unwritten between the lines of the text.

These chapters also evoke the consideration of the definition of justice in society, especially capital punishment. The idea that certain men who are born without a human conscience deserve death is introduced. The fact that the Captain is able to sleep well after the gunfight, when previously in his history, during war, he was unable to sleep after combat, infers that his sleeplessness before was due to a guilty conscience, and having to kill men who were innocent, or at the very least, soldiers like himself. However, after the shoot-out and death of Almay, he can sleep because he has saved a young girl from the clutches of a man who wanted to exploit her sexually, for his own monetary gain, something that is inarguably deplorable, referencing a thought of his from Chapter 4: "More than ever knowing in his fragile bones that it was the duty of men who aspired to the condition of humanity to protect children and kill for them if necessary" (38). The Captain has done his duty, has done a good thing.

Chapters 14-18

Chapter 14 Summary

As they arrive in Durand, the Captain bargains with the owner of a broom-and-stave mill about allowing them to stay the night in the loading yard. The man asks for 50¢, an exorbitant price, the Captain finds, but without many options, he pays.

The Captain readies himself for business and tries to teach Johanna how to tell time. He believes she understands and leaves his watch with her.

He tacks up his handbills everywhere. Street urchins follow him around, which annoys him. He knows they can't read and goads them by telling them that his placards say he is going to saw a very fat woman in half. He tells them to leave him alone, and they quickly grow bored and leave. A little later on, after placing handbills in several other key locations, he gives a well-dressed man one of them personally. The man appears intrigued and asks the Captain will he also be reading from the *Daily State Journal*, which the Captain vehemently denies he will do, touting the journal as mere propaganda. This offends the man. After some bickering back and forth, the Captain tells the man to just stay home if he doesn't want to hear non-political news.

Back at the broom mill, Johanna is off tending to things while the Captain is looking through his papers. He is trying to find articles that will "soothe" the crowd. The narrator points out, once again, that all of the papers he carries are devoid of anything about the political situation in Texas. The broom man accosts the Captain about the girl, stating that there is something "off" about her. The Captain doesn't feel like discussing her with the man. The Captain bemoans to himself about the tough situation he is in, taking care of Johanna, fighting off bad men who want to do unspeakable things with her, earning enough money to survive, and avoiding the brutal clashes of Texan politics. Eventually, he tells the man to just mind his own business.

While he's sitting on the tailgate of the wagon, trying to relax, he hears Johanna's telltale Kiowa shouting, along with that of another woman's, coming from the direction of the river. He grabs Johanna's poncho, knowing what the problem is. At the river, he finds Johanna naked, running away from a young woman who is chasing her and screaming "[w]e cannot have naked bathing here" (137). Johanna takes refuge in a hole near the bank. The Captain comes to her and explains to the woman Johanna's situation, guilting the woman for treating Johanna so harshly. He tells the woman that a Christian would be trying to find food and clothing for a girl like Johanna, rather than chasing her and scaring her. He takes her back to the wagon. She is barefoot, hurt, angry, and despairing.

It's now 8pm and the Captain is tucking Johanna in for the night. He changes into his reading clothes. He talks to her for a bit, telling her how he will go off and read and bring home the bacon, that the citizens of Durand will pay him well. He regards her with tenderness, thinking how she can burst into tears one moment and in another be bright with energy and laughter. He wants to kiss her on the cheek, but doesn't know whether or not that is allowed in Kiowa culture, so he simply pats the air and tells her to "[s]it. Stay" (140).

Chapter 15 Summary

People file into the mercantile store to listen to the Captain read. A US Army sergeant guards the door and has people remove any arms they are carrying. The Captain tries not to look into their faces, but can't help noticing them from the corner of his eyes. He notices how they divide themselves into two groups. As he reads, he is interrupted from time to time with people expressing their political opinions. He is able to silence the interruptions with his stentorian voice, that is until two gentlemen, the owner of the hotel and the schoolteacher, come to blows. A brouhaha ensues. The Captain's dime can is knocked over and merchandise is broken. People leave the store to escape the fight. The fight quickly moves outdoors with the rest of the crowd.

The Captain remains in the disheveled store. He bends down to gather his scattered dimes, which he wouldn't have done, on account of his pride, if he wasn't having to take care of Johanna. A man tells him that he shouldn't have to do that. It's the black-bearded man from earlier. He offers the Captain a chair, introduces himself as John Calley, and begins gathering the coins for him. John is ashamed and remorseful about what he and his brother and cousins had done earlier to the Captain and Johanna, and he regrets further having taken his money. The two of them have a discussion about law. John defends his actions with the fact that, in the current situation, the definition of what is lawful and what isn't is fluid. At one point, the Captain asks John if he is interested in "reading" the law, meaning becoming a lawyer. John adamantly denies that he wants to do that. He then, however, asks where one might begin learning of the law, if one were so inclined. The Captain ends their conversation by quoting a part of the Code of Hammurabi.

Just as in Dallas, the Captain realizes it's best if he and Johanna get out of town as quickly as possible. He didn't have a chance to buy any ammunition or get the wagon's wheel fixed. He simply goes back to the mill, readies the horses and wagon, and goes to Johanna. She is delighted to see him. She shows him the nice clothes the "bad water" woman brought her. The Captain muses on the good of stricken consciences. While he is distracted with the final preparations to leave, Johanna ducks into the shed, emerges, and jumps up onto the wagon, carrying a burlap sack. He's too worried thinking about what might come at them next along their route to check what it is she has.

Later on, Johanna retrieves the sack and proudly shows him what she has brought. It happens to be the two chickens from the stave mill owner, his two pet chickens (he named them Penelope and Amelia). She's happy about what she's done and sets about preparing a roast-chicken breakfast. The Captain is beside himself with pity for her and once again thinks about how hard it will be for her to adjust to a new life with her relatives in Castroville. He sheds a few tears. Johanna notices him crying and wipes his tears with a blood-sticky hand. She tells him he's hungry and sets back to work. He tells her that old people just cry easily. She asks if everything's alright. He tells her everything is indeed alright.

Chapter 16 Summary

They travel a good ways before coming to Cranfills Gap, where they stop for a time. They eat the chickens and rest. The Captain has an odd dream about an armed, foul-smelling man rising out of the Leon River that looks part amphibian and part human. Disturbing dreams are something that always happens to him after conflict. He remembers that his wife, Maria, used to climb out of bed while he was having a nightmare and whisper calming words to him. The Captain wonders if it's the violence of being forcefully taken from their parents that make the returned children so odd. They remain in Cranfills Gap the entire next day, as the Captain needs rest.

The pair make it twenty miles the following day. While they travel, he continues to teach Johanna English. She continues making progress. She can now count to 100, lace her shoes (when he can get her to actually wear them), and she can sing the song, "Hard Times." The terrain is very open and solitary. He feels how alone they are. He thinks back to when he left for North Texas, a year after Maria had died. He thinks back on the time he first met her, back when he had his own printing press, and how much he loved putting words to paper. He is angry at the fact that when people die, they never send messages back from the beyond.

They come upon an elderly woman, alone, driving a wagon. She has come from Lampasas, where he and

Johanna are heading. She is on her way to Durand. The Captain asks the woman to take two 50-cent pieces to the owner of the stave mill. The man doesn't have a good reputation with the woman, and so she wants to refuse, but the Captain convinces her to do it for him, because he doesn't want to be known as a chicken thief. She can understand that, and thus acquiesces.

Shortly after the episode with the woman, the Captain switches to riding the other horse, Pasha, alongside the wagon, because they are in unfriendly country. He places a blanket on top of the saddle for extra cushion. He enjoys the ride and can't help but pat the horse's neck from time to time and play with its mane. The Captain knows that there is a lot of trouble in Lampasas. He had passed through years earlier and knows that there is an ongoing feud between two families there. He remarks on the increase in traffic as they get closer to the town, and he wonders if people from the region come into town on Saturdays to shop or spend the day, drink, and wait to go to church on Sunday. Spring is in the air.

Four men on horseback are blocking the road. Johanna retreats inside her poncho. The Captain recognizes the men as cowboys because of the equipment they carry. He dismounts and stands near Johanna to try and keep her calm. The four men have come to warn him about the Horrell brothers in Lampasas. They advise him against doing a reading there. Apparently, the Horrell brothers aren't very intelligent; they're wild, and they have it in their minds that the eastern papers (New York, Philadelphia, etc.) will have stories about them because they heard that the papers back east have been reporting on cowboys. The four men—who are the Merritt brothers, and have heard the Captain read before in the town of Meridian and respect him—tell him that when the Horrells discover

36

they aren't mentioned in any papers, they're going to cause trouble. The Captain thanks them several times. During the conversation, the men sometimes curse and then tip their hats to Johanna, excusing themselves for using uncouth language. Johanna is unsettled by their gestures, unsure of their meaning.

The Captain climbs back atop Pasha, feeling good about his physical condition at the age of 71. He then realizes that he's 72, that his birthday was yesterday, the 15th of March. He thinks back on his 16th birthday and remembers that at that time he couldn't have imagined living so long, and definitely not doing what he is now, at such an old age.

Chapter 17 Summary

The Captain decides he will just avoid the Horrells at all costs. However, the Horrell brothers track him down, and watch him and Johanna unload their wagon. They approach him and ask if he's the man who reads the news. He confirms that he is. They want to know why they aren't in the news. He tells them he does not know because he isn't the one who writes the papers. There is further bantering back and forth and the Captain sizes the Horrell brothers up for exactly what the Merritt brothers told him about them. The Horrells boast about their having killed many Mexicans. The Captain asks them if no one objects to them killing Mexicans. They think maybe the soldiers might, but there aren't any around. They don't seem worried or care. They really want to know if they are mentioned in the news, and the Captain feeds them hope in order to keep them calm, saying that they just might be for all he knows. They invite the Captain to come and read the news at The Gem saloon that evening. The Captain thanks them and asks if it will be alright if he's a little late. They say that's fine and ride off.

The Captain has no intention of going and stays up late. He can hear music and shouting and figures it's the Horrell brothers, getting drunk. He doesn't sleep all night. He notices a glowing cigarette in the distance and knows it's one of the Merritt brothers from earlier, keeping their word that they would keep an eye on him and Johanna, making sure nothing bad befalls them.

Chapter 18 Summary

The Captain and Johanna are deeper in hill country now. The Captain rides with his butcher knife and revolver in his waistband. He has a plan in case raiders show up: he will cut the packhorse out of the harness, throw Johanna on the saddle, which he has already placed on the packhorse, and make a run for it, hoping the deserted wagon will be all the raiders are interested in.

Both of them are very alert and wary of their surroundings. Johanna doesn't play anymore, sing, or make up nonsense English sentences. She helps the Captain listen for trouble. They come across abandoned farms, some having been burned down. They stop at one to take a break. They step inside the farmhouse, and the Captain removes a .50-caliber bullet from the wall. He imagines what life was like on that farm, before whatever happened to it transpired. There is a spring nearby and so they plan on staying for the night. Johanna needs a swim and a bath with soap. The Captain ties the horses in a shady place, and he and Johanna sit in the shade of the springhouse. From there, they have a good vantage point of the surrounding area.

All of a sudden, the Captain notices the branch of a large oak tree shutter. A slim, young man drops from the branches. He has long blond hair with one side cut very short, a marking of the Kiowa. More men drop behind him from the tree. He begins to wonder if Johanna will betray him and call out to the Kiowa, because that is what she has wanted since being with him, he assumes, going back to the Kiowa and the life she knew. She places her hand on his arm and neither of them say anything. The Kiowa move off into the distance.

The Captain and Johanna continue on south towards Castroville, stopping in the German town of Fredericksburg. As usual, the Captain rents two rooms at the hotel, one for him and one for Johanna. The townspeople have heard about Johanna from Bianca Babb, who had brought his own granddaughter back from Indian territory. The town people warn the Captain about how odd those who return are. He offers to do a reading in town, but he's sure few will show up since most of the town's population doesn't speak English and is not interested in faraway news. He considers it a practice session to see how well Johanna can sit still and collect the dimes. He tries to finally get the wagon wheel fixed, but the local blacksmith has been killed on the road to Kerriville.

Before the reading, the Captain and Johanna eat a German meal of noodles, mutton, and a cream sauce in their hotel rooms. Her manners are much improved. She is happy to make him pleased. She slurps a noodle up quickly so that it smacks her on the nose. She laughs so hard tears form in her eyes. The Captain thinks about how nice it is to have a homecooked meal and not have to clean the dishes afterwards.

The Captain is able to secure the *Vereins Kirche*, or People's Church, and he places Johanna near the entrance with the dime can. He does a practice round with her before the main event. She does very well that evening, even finding the German word *Achtung* to shout when a man goes past her without paying.

After the reading, he and Johanna walk back to the hotel hand in hand. He tucks her in and she quickly falls asleep. He cleans the revolver and makes a list: "feed, flour, ammunition, soup, beef, faith, hope, charity" (177).

Chapters 14-18 Analysis

Johanna's English language skills continue to develop; however, her syntax, vocabulary, and pronunciation are still very rudimentary. We have already come across words in Kiowa, German, Spanish and even Gaelic, and even though Johanna has never spoken English well or correctly, the fact that she is the only character whose accent is written out phonetically becomes, in these chapters, far more pronounced against the background of language as a thematic element.

The Captain, for example, was born and raised in Georgia, only to then move to Texas. One can safely assume that he speaks with a southern accent in one form or another. However, his dialogue is never written out phonetically, nor are the accents of any other characters—no one except for Johanna. This not only illustrates her difficulty in speaking and understanding English, but also separates her from everyone else, making her an anomaly. Not only does the narration, the descriptions of her character, of others regarding the problems of returned captives, and her constant hiding inside the *jorongo* single her out as an outsider, and someone belonging to no culture, creed, or country, the text completely isolates her linguistically as well, proof of her singularity and peculiarity.

From the very beginning, but heavily reinforced in Chapter 15, the political turmoil of post-war Texas echoes the political environment of contemporary US politics. The extreme polarization of the two differing sides is starkly highlighted in the mercantile store when the town's population divides itself according to their respective political camps. In a politically-divided, contemporary America, the reader is provided a blatant scene of intolerance, resulting in physical violence between two people of the community that one would expect to maintain civility during any sort of discussion: a business owner and a schoolteacher. The scene provides an opportunity for reflection on the nature of political discussions.

The Captain's strict sense of honor and morals is illustrated in his strong desire to make amends for Johanna having taken the chickens from the stave mill owner, a man whom the Captain clearly doesn't like. But his reputation and sense of duty requires him to reimburse the man for the misappropriation of his chickens, paying a price far above their actual worth.

Chapter 19-22

Chapter 19 Summary

The Captain and Johanna arrive in the town of Bandera. There are teams of oxen in the street: it's a line of freight wagons that will leave the town together as protection against the Comanche. The Captain reads new stories, stories about how Texas has recently been readmitted to the Union, the building of the Brooklyn Bridge, the Cincinnati Reds as the first professional baseball team. Johanna is no longer afraid of large crowds of white people, and so she sits in the back with the paint can to collect the dimes. She threatens anyone who attempts to go by her without paying.

They are in the lower country now, having descended from the hills. The weather is warm. The Captain remembers the territory; it's a part of him, and will never not be. The wind and smells remind him of his old home, his wife, war, and watching his captain die in his arms, those many years ago. Johanna senses a change coming and she grows uneasy. She speaks of the doll she left overlooking the Red River. She asks if they will be reading in Castroville, to which the Captain answers no, not anymore. He tells her he's taking her to her aunt and uncle. She tries to play with him, tears running down her face. He tells her she will adjust, using a firm voice, tells her it would be dishonorable of him to not take her to her relatives after he had promised he would.

Castroville is a small town with a European aesthetic. The Captain asks people in town where Wilhelm and Anna Leonberger live. He does not mention anything about Johanna. The townspeople do, however, mention Johanna and her parents, and inform him that her parents are buried in the cemetery of Saint Dominic's. They pass the graveyard and the Captain removes his hat as he had been taught to do. Johanna regards them with curiosity, but mostly indifference. She tells the Captain she wants to go back to Dallas, that she doesn't like Castroville. He tells her they cannot. She reverts to her Kiowa ways, chants a Kiowa aphorism, braids her hair as if she were preparing for war, and becomes wooden and silent.

Along the route, the Captain asks a man, Adolph, for directions, telling him he will pay him if he rides up ahead and announces to the Leonbergers Johanna's arrival. The man praises God and rushes off.

They arrive at the Leonberger farm. The Captain climbs down from the wagon. Adolph is waiting in front of the house. Dogs run out barking. A man emerges from the cabin and shoos the dogs away. The Captain feels very tired. Anna emerges and stands beside Wilhelm. The Captain announces that he has brought Johanna back and hands Wilhelm the papers from the Agent. Wilhelm doesn't say anything and simply reads over the papers. He then tells the Captain that he sent $50. The Captain confirms he received it, adding that with the money he had bought the wagon. Wilhelm asks if he also bought the harness with the money. The Captain says he did. Wilhelm wants to know if he has a receipt. The Captain tells him that no, he does not. Wilhelm reluctantly invites them inside. Adolph bites his lip in dismay and then rides off.

Chapter 20 Summary

The Captain realizes the futility of explaining Johanna's situation to the Leonbergers—that is, that she needs an adjustment period—while sitting on their sofa, drinking a very strong coffee. Johanna, meanwhile, is in a corner of the room, sitting on her haunches, holding her ankles.

Wilhelm and Anna tell the Captain in broken English of how Johanna's parents were killed, in grizzly detail. He only responds with simple affirmations of having understood. Anna tells Johanna to get up, but she ignores him and remains in the corner. They begin discussing her. Wilhelm states that she needs to be retaught their ways, that she needs to work, that they need a lot of help around the farm. The Captain agrees that she can work, but asks Wilhelm and Anna to bear in mind everything Johanna has been through, and to not be harsh on her. Wilhelm asks about the receipt again.

The Captain spends the night on a hard bed upstairs in the Leonberger home. Johanna remains in the wagon, wrapped up in her poncho.

The next day, the town gathers to see Johanna. She retreats into the hayloft in the barn and throws things at anyone who attempts to approach her. The Captain tells the people to just please leave her alone for a little while.

Later on, the town gathers together to celebrate Johanna's return. They are kind, well-meaning, and hard-working people. The celebration is filled with wonderful foods from the Alsatian region of France/Germany, along with Texas-style brisket. Adolph, the messenger, comes over and sits down with the Captain. Adolph tells him about the Leonbergers, and that their nephew had run away. The Captain accurately deduces that he ran away because the Leonbergers overworked him. Adolph and the Captain muse over the fact that the people from the town celebrate Johanna's return, but afterwards, no one will stop by and check up on her welfare. Adolph briefly mentions how he had done what he could to chase down Johanna's kidnappers. He mentions to the Captain about adoption papers, and that Wilhelm and Anna will not adopt Johanna because of the legal responsibilities that would come with it. The Captain notices that the Leonbergers sit alone at the festivities, and that no one goes over and speaks with them. Adolph informs him that Wilhelm and Anna hadn't adopted their nephew, either. Adolph takes the Captain by the sleeve and very poignantly tells him that he cannot leave Johanna with them. The Captain says he will try and visit, and then quickly leaves before tears start running down his face.

Chapter 21 Summary

The Captain returns to Castroville (the Leonbergers actually live in the small village of D'Hanis, twenty-two miles away), and stays the night in the hotel there. From there, he travels to San Antonio. He is very happy to be back. He loves the city and its river. He looks in the windows of the old building where he used to have his printing shop. He stops in at Branholme's law office and spends thirty minutes discussing adoption, the legal status of returned captives, and the Printing Bill. Branholme does not provide a very positive outlook regarding adoption, and he hopes that in a few years Governor Davis will rescind the bill, so that the Captain can reopen his printing shop.

From there, the Captain checks for mail at the post office and reads a letter from his daughter, Elizabeth. She states they will come back in two years, and states the difficulties they would have traveling to San Antonio. She tells him that if he has money he could send them some, that it would be very helpful. He also purchases more newspapers, though he will not be doing a reading in San Antonio. His readings are only popular in the small towns in the north and west of Texas. He has a room at The Vance House and pays a boy to go out and bring him back a pint of whiskey. He ruminates in the night that he is neither a cripple nor stupid.

The next morning he travels back to the Leonberger farm. He wants to explain Johanna's situation, her state of mind, to them, and get them to treat her well. He will do what it takes, whether that means reason, bribery, or something else. It is night by the time he arrives. He stops underneath a mesquite tree. He notices a light on in the farmhouse window. Then he notices Johanna, alone, walking among the grasses, carrying heavy leather halters and feed for the horses. She calls to the horses in Kiowa. He calls out her name. She stops and stares back at the wagon. He notices she is dirty and still wearing the same dress as when he dropped her off last. He's angry that the Leonbergers haven't provided her new clothing. She calls out his name and comes over to feed Pasha. It's the only way she can think of to make herself welcomed. He notices dark red stripes across her arms and hands from the dog whip. The anger he feels freezes him in place. He tells her, calmly, to drop everything and come along with him. She drops it all and jumps over the fence and comes running to him. She's crying and saying she will go with him. They head north. The Captain says that if anyone has a problem with him taking her, then they will shoot them full of dimes.

Chapter 22 Summary

Over the next several years, the Captain and Johanna travel all over Texas, reading the news. He teaches her to read and write. She learns English well, but continually speaks with an accent that is not Texan and struggles with the pronunciation of the letter r. She never learns to value what white people value, and he notices that he has learned from her to value those things less as well. He becomes more and more interested in foreign news. He never does figure out what made Johanna change so drastically over those four years with the Kiowa, but knows that she remains Kiowa at heart and will until the end of her days.

After three years, his daughters move to San Antonio. His son-in-law opens a printing press. The Captain helps out. They all live in the old Betancort house and Elizabeth works at recovering the rest of the Spanish lands of her mother's family. Olympia drifts for a while but eventually remarries.

One day, John Calley, who always remembered the Captain from Durand and respected him, pays him a visit. By this time, Johanna is 15 years old and has transformed into a southern belle. Calley stays with them for a while and he courts Johanna. They grow to like one another. John undertakes a difficult project of obtaining cattle from the wild country, but because he is tough and resourceful, he becomes a "made-man" within just two trips. He and Johanna eventually marry.

In their last scene together, she and the Captain sit on her bed and talk. She cries. She is worried about marriage, and in familiar words, he calms her. Just as when she was with him during the readings, and it was time for him to read, she looks down at his watch and announces it's time to go. They embrace. She says she will visit, and tells him that he is her "cuuative watah" (208).

Johanna and John make a living driving cattle. It's a life she can love. They live into the 20th century and have two children.

The Captain grows older, but still remembers the shootout he had with Johanna at his side.

Britt Johnson and his crew are killed in 1871 by Comanches while they are driving freight. Simon and Doris have a family of six children, all their names beginning with "D," and travel north Texas as musicians.

The Captain dies, and in his will he requests to be buried with his runner's badge from 1814: "He said he had message to deliver, contents unknown (209)."

Chapters 19-22 Analysis

The climax of finally reaching their destination after many miles and adventures together comes to a head in Chapter 19. The Leonbergers turn out to be exactly what the Captain feared all along: people ill-prepared or unwilling to understand the fragile state-of-mind Johanna is in. However, as established in earlier chapters, the Captain's sense of duty and honor is so strong that he reluctantly fulfills his task and rides away, fighting back tears. However, his sense of honor and moral code are facing a paradox, as he knows that Johanna will not be okay with her aunt and uncle, and he feels the strong desire to save her from a terrible fate. Ultimately, his love for Johanna, and sense of what is right, trumps everything else.

Interesting to note is the juxtaposition of the Adolph character with that of the Leonbergers. The Leonbergers represent the humorless, cold, bureaucratic Germans, the ones who are solely interested in hard work and business, caring more for receipts and paperwork than their niece. Adolph, on the other hand, represents the Germans who are more loving and caring, going so far to inform the Captain to take Johanna away. In their discussions, a weakness of all cultures and peoples is raised which further solidifies the idea that no one country, people, or culture is superior or inferior to any other, that they all share the fault of not caring properly for children, that they all comprised of good and bad individuals.

Captain Jefferson Kyle Kidd

The Captain is the protagonist of the novel, the glue that
holds everything and everyone together. He is 72 years old
for much of the novel's narrative present. His birthday is on
March 15. He was born and raised in Georgia. He is an
educated, well-read man. He loves the printed word, and
after having suffered the loss of his own printing press
because of the Civil War, he travels Texas reading US and
international news to people who cannot read and/or live in
small, isolated areas of Texas. He is a man who has fought
in two wars: the first in 1812, when he was only 16, and the
second being the Mexican-American war. Thus, he is no
stranger to violence and battle, though he avoids it as best
he can. However, when push comes to shove, he is not a
man to be taken lightly. He was married, but his wife has
already passed. He has two daughters.

Captain Kidd embodies the frontier, wild-west spirit of the
quintessential Texan towards the end of the 19th century,
but these traits are combined with the civility and education
of an open-minded gentleman. He is tough, ingenious,
loves freedom, his family, and lives by a strict code of
honor. He possess many virtues but virtually no vices,
especially the ones common during this era, such as
drunkenness and gambling.

He is a Southerner through and through, and he was a
supporter of the Confederacy. Perhaps because of this,
though it is never directly addressed, he possesses a sense
of white guilt with regards to African Americans. The
reason for this assumption is that he admits that the reason
he had first agreed to take Johanna to her family was for
Britt Johnson, "a freed black man" (86). This could also

just speak to his honor, and trying to do something good for someone who had suffered social injustices earlier, and who, because of current animosity towards freed former slaves, recognizes it was easier for him than for Britt. Either way, out of personal or collective guilt, something draws the Captain to Britt Johnson, more so than with any other freed black man.

Johanna Leonberger

Johanna is the second most important character, and her fate and ordeal sets the momentum of the plot. Her Kiowa name is Cicada, and she identifies much more with Native culture than she does with white culture. She is the mediator of two very different worlds in the book. She is the mirror that reflects white American culture, causing contemplation of itself and its own vales and customs. She also illustrates the difficulty in walking the line between two worlds, and what it is like to be an outsider, someone who is not fully accepted into any society, culture, or group. She is neither 100% Kiowa nor Anglo-American.

Johanna is a very hearty and tough individual. She is ingenuous, which she displays with her idea to use the dimes in the shotgun. She is battle-hardened, like the Captain, even though she is only 10 years old. She is somewhat emotionally unstable in that she can collapse into tears one minute and in the next be as hard as stone. She is clearly insecure and distrusting of others, shown in the way she cowers underneath her poncho when strangers are nearby, though if she feels threatened she will fight or run. Above all, she is extremely adaptable. Though she struggles, she manages to reintegrate into American society. It is, of course, with the excellent and loving care and help of the Captain that she is able to do this, but her strength of character, which she displays several times throughout the story, is firm.

John Calley

Calley is a young man caught up in the wildness of post-war Texas. He is somewhat political and interested in legal matters. He engages the Captain in a legal discussion after the Durand fiasco, and he helps the Captain gather coins. He is penitent and apologetic for his earlier behavior, which shows that he is a good man at heart, forced to do bad things in extraneous circumstances. He cleans up his ways, eventually making a good living in south Texas raising cattle, and becomes a good husband for Johanna, providing her with a life balanced between the freedom of nature, on cattle drives and American civilized society, which is important for her continued happiness.

Wilhelm and Anna Leonberger

The Leonbergers are German immigrants who have settled in the D'Hanis/Castroville, Texas area. They are a terse couple possessing the exaggerated, stereotypical characteristics of the uptight, anal-retentive Prussian. When the Captain delivers Johanna, there is no display of emotion, especially from Wilhelm, who is more interested in the Agent's paperwork and whether or not the Captain has a receipt of sale for the wagon he bought with the money Wilhelm had sent for Johanna's safe return, than he is with Johanna's welfare. The two are abusive to Johanna and the Captain eventually rescues the girl from them.

Maria Luisa Betancort y Real

Maria is the Captain's late wife, and came from an old Spanish family in the San Antonio region. Her family lands are tied up in Texas/US bureaucratic red tape, so that the Captain doesn't have access to them. The text hints at the fact that she was a loving wife and mother, but little is actually told about her.

Elizabeth and Olympia

Elizabeth is the younger daughter of the Captain and Maria. She is married and the more industrious of the two. It's her task to wade through the legalities of getting her mother's lands back.

Olympia is widowed and living with Elizabeth and her husband, Emory, and has struggled since then. She remarries at the end, and lives a happy life.

Britt Johnson

Johnson is a freed black man that earns his money by hauling freight around the state. His son was kidnapped by the Kiowa, but through a means no one knows, he has an innate ability to sneak into a camp and rescue captives. He rescued his son, and rescues others as well from time to time. He is a good friend to the Captain. He seeks the Captain's help, but also does what he can to make things better for him, giving him his own pistol to take along, something that is against the law and would mean that he is now not as well-armed for his own treacherous journey. He and his men are killed in a Comanche raid at the end of the novel.

Simon Boudlin

Simon is a fiddler in the town of Red River and a friend of the Captain's. He, with his girlfriend, Doris, watch over Johanna while the Captain does a reading. He also helps the

Captain find her after she runs off (while Simon was watching her, it should be added). He marries Doris and they have six children together. Together, the family forms a musical group.

Doris Dillon

Doris is an Irish woman who can easily sympathize with Johanna's plight because she knows what it's like to be of two different worlds—i.e., to be Irish and American, not quite one or the other, but rather a mixture of both. She even tells the Captain that he can leave Johanna with them, permanently, and that they will take care of her.

Almay

At first, Almay is simply known as the pale-haired man. Later, he introduces himself and we learn his name. He is the narrative's antagonist, and is so bad that his evil surprises the Captain. Almay is a pimp who prostitutes underage girls and wants to purchase Johanna from the Captain. He travels with two Caddos Indians who are his hired muscle. When the Captain refuses to sell Johanna to him and runs, Almay chases them down and begins a gunfight to try and take her from him. He is shot dead by one of the Captain's and Johanna's improvised, dime-filled shotgun shells.

The Horrell Brothers

The Horrell Brothers are Merritt, Tom, Mart, Benjamin, and Sam. They are basically a representation of wild, uneducated, uncouth, barbarous frontier cowboy types. They enjoy hunting down and killing Mexicans, something which they believe is a good thing, and feel that they should be written about in the newspapers. The Captain is warned about them by the Merritt brothers. The Horrell and Merritt brothers are sons of two families that are feuding.

The Merritt Brothers

These brothers are the antithesis of the Horrell brothers, and they are juxtaposed against the Horrells as a counterbalance to display the characteristics of good cowboys. They left their herd to personally warn the Captain about the Horrells causing trouble. They also take turns watching over the Captain and Johanna to make sure the Horrells don't come around and bother them. It's interesting to note that the eldest Horrell carries the family name of the enemy family as his first (that is, Merritt Horrell).

Mrs. Gannet

Gannet is an attractive, 45-year-old widow, with a thin, girlish waist. She lives in Dallas. She owns and runs a livery stable. The Captain is romantically interested in her, but doesn't call upon her because of his daughters, whom he believes would find it as an effrontery to their mother's memory. Despite the Captain's intentions to ask her on a date later, they never get together, and she eventually marries another man, and remains in Dallas.

Adolph

Adolph is a German immigrant and acquaintance of Wilhelm and Anna Leonberger. He recognizes the poor conditions that Wilhelm and Anna provide, working their nephew too hard, and he warns the Captain of this, ultimately telling him that he can't leave Johanna with them.

THEMES

The Importance of News and the Written Word

The titular theme of the novel runs throughout the book, from the very first page to the very last. The Captain's explicit *raison d'être* is to deliver messages, tales, and news from around the world to isolated communities in Texas. As a teenager, he discovers the importance of being a messenger during wartime, stating that "written information was what mattered in this world" (22). The recognition and love of written information motivates him after the war to open his own printing press. Even with the subsequent loss of his press, caused by the Civil War, it doesn't keep him from continuing his life's mission of spreading and delivering messages.

The importance of news is not solely relegated to the Captain, however. The very fact that he can make money reading to people illustrates their desire for information and stories. It has a calming and healing effect on them: "the listeners would for a small space of time drift away into a healing place like curative waters" (30). Even though there are many positive aspects to the power of the written word, there are also negative ones, ones of which the Captain is very aware, which is portrayed in the propagandistic literature supplied by Governor Davis and his state journal.

Furthermore, news provides an element of objectivism against which people can measure their own lives and worlds. By listening to news from faraway places like Europe and India, Texans are offered a broader perspective when considering the world. They can realize that war and destruction takes place around the globe—for example, The Franco-Prussian War—or that the expansion of the railroads is bringing people from far away closer together, and can marvel at the invention of the telegraph.

Linguistic and Cultural Differences

Though the novel is written in English, the English language itself, in the plot of the narrative, doesn't necessarily carry with it more importance than any other language. Rather, it comes across as being a trade language, or a language for unification/point-of-commonality's sake. The character who is the most educated, the Captain, is a man who is familiar with several languages: Spanish (which he speaks at an advanced level), Plains Sign Language (novice), Kiowa (novice), and German (novice). In fact, while in Durand, the Captain describes his disgust and frustration with the mill owner, whose command of the English language is tentative, and that he does not possess the ability to recognize his own lingual limitations: "The fool sat there and [...] considered himself an expert on the English language because it spilled out of his mouth [...] and he didn't even have to think about it" (136).

Furthermore, the Captain's familiarity with other languages reinforces one of the Captain's strongest and most important characteristics: his open-mindedness and understanding and tolerance with cultures and ways different than his own, which is something one can argue is directly related to his knowledge of language and exposure and experience dealing with others.

Even though Johanna is a character torn between two worlds, it's her multilingual abilities that help her acclimate to new surroundings and even move between the two. Her mind is flexible and open. From a very young age, she learned that there is more than one way to express herself, and more than one name for a physical object. This is an aspect that makes both her and the Captain very three-dimensional characters, rather than the other two-dimensional characters who can only speak one language, or are only familiar with one worldview. Language, then, is a bridge to culture and understanding others.

Nature Versus Civilization

The Kiowa represent a people with a strong and close relationship to nature. The white European-Americans represent the contrary, a people who use and manipulate their environment for their own designs, and who even invent behaviors and mannerisms completely separate from nature. The two different societies are consistently juxtaposed in the novel, without either one truly gaining an upper hand. Both have their advantages and disadvantages. The Kiowa portray a purer, spiritual, and mystic culture that is very atavistic, living very simple lives, and trying to live in harmony with their natural surroundings. Of course, this means that technological advances as simple as printed/written language and the wheel are sacrificed for such a lifestyle. The European-Americans, by contrast, have all the advantages of civilization, but there is a gap created by the separation of man from the natural world, a gap that Johanna is never able to fully bridge, implying that the atavistic connection to the earth is not an easy one to severe once it has been formed.

The Family and Home

The role that family plays in the novel is bound with the sense of belonging. The Captain, though born and raised in Georgia, considers San Antonio home because that is where he met his wife, Maria, and where they raised their daughters. Instead of returning to Georgia to be with his daughters and son-in-law, he wants them to move out to

Texas, ostensibly because he feels there are better economic opportunities, but the memory of his late wife cannot be devalued.

For Johanna, family is also important. She lost her biological parents, whom she can barely remember. Furthermore, the need for belonging, family, and home is so strong that it doesn't seem that she is able to remember their demise at the hands of her new, adoptive Kiowa family, for whom she pines after being separated from them. Also, if she can remember it was the Kiowa who killed them, she doesn't seem too concerned with it.

Despite her tenuous history with family, it is nevertheless something she desires, and even requires, and which she eventually finds in the Captain, and later with John Calley, with whom she builds a family of her own. With Johanna, each family she is with leaves an indelible impression upon her: she retains some knowledge of the German language from her first parents, and the ways of the Kiowa are so ingrained in her that she never fully forgets them. Additionally, the love and care that the Captain gives her is ultimately what saves her and allows her to reintegrate into American culture.

Justice

Myriad subtopics of justice emerge throughout the novel: the taking and returning of captives, Reconstruction issues/martial law, frontier justice/lawlessness, the Code of Hammurabi, adoption laws, and child abuse. The issue with captives was difficult and its solutions tenuous at best. The Indian tribes followed a different moral code than Anglo-Americans, and there was so much animosity and war throughout that period that captives were often treated much like POWs, rather than kidnapping victims.

Reconstruction was also a mess. The Southern states were very often unhappy with their treatment by the victorious North, and US politicians were often at odds on how exactly to punish and/or readmit the Southern states to the US. Some, like Abraham Lincoln and Andrew Johnson, sought lenient terms and desired a quick return. However, some wanted to see the South severely punished for their rebellion. The transition of former slaves, who forever and legally were freed by the Fifteenth Amendment, was obviously very difficult and fraught with tension.

As the book illustrates, the tremendous task of policing the sparsely-populated regions of Texas (and the rest of the American frontier) often resulted in people taking matters into their own hands. The shootout with Almay, and the Horrell brothers killing Mexicans without any repercussions, display how violent things could be. The scene with John Calley, where he and his cousins exact a toll for free, unmolested passage into Durand, and then John Calley's subsequent remorse, raise the question as to what kept areas without official law from devolving into complete anarchy. The Captain brings up the Code of Hammurabi, but Christian values are also subtly hinted at.

Towards the end of the book, with the whole problematic relationship between Johanna and her aunt and uncle, the issue of adoption and child welfare emerges. The abusing aunt and uncle legally have guardianship over Johanna, and the Captain has no legal recourse to remove her from them, even though he cares about her, and treats her well and fairly, loves her as a daughter even.

Memory

The trouble and beauty of memory runs throughout the novel. Johanna struggles with the memories she has of her biological parents being murdered at the hands of the Kiowa, and the memories of life among the Kiowa are so strong that she is never able to fully forget, which causes her to forever remain Kiowa at heart.

The Captain carries the memories of war, especially his time as a messenger during the War of 1812. He also remembers his wife, Maria, which are such fond memories that he struggles with thinking about her because the pain of her passing is still very much with him.

Newspapers

Newspapers are the physical manifestations of knowledge and the power of the written word, and the means of accessing the outside world, broadening the mind and one's familiarity with and understanding of distant places and other peoples and cultures. They also symbolize the Captain's desire for peace among the people of Texas. The Captain believes that if people understand more of the world, they are less likely to come to violent action.

The Curative Waters Wagon

The wagon is not only the Captain's and Johanna's means of transportation, but also symbol for the healing process of the two characters. The entire journey is a journey of healing, for both the Captain and Johanna. Johanna states at the end of the novel that she is the Captain's "curative waters." Early in the novel, it's said that the Captain's "life seemed to him thin and sour, a bit spoiled" (3), yet the longer he spends with Johanna, the better his life becomes, despite the hardships involved with transporting her across the state.

Johanna's Jorongo

A jorongo is a Mexican-Spanish word for a poncho/serape. The jorongo becomes Johanna's security blanket, the space between the cloth, a place of refuge in times of trouble, or when she feels insecure, which happens almost always when strangers approach the wagon. It is interesting to note the choice of word. Jorongo is a specific word for an article of clothing, and the adopted word in English is poncho, but Johanna doesn't seek comfort from an English word, but rather from a non-English foreign word. The fact that an article of Mexican clothing has become adopted garb for white people, and the fact that Johanna herself was taken from European-American culture and thrust into Native American culture, before re-entering Anglo-American culture, illustrates the intersectionality of cultures in Texas.

The Broken Wagon Wheel

The wagon wheel on the Captain's wagon breaks very early, and though the Captain wants to get it repaired, he never does until he reaches the end of the journey. The wheel, then, becomes a metaphor for Johanna herself. She is broken, too, and needing repairing (healing), and it takes the entire journey for her to achieve this process.

Weather

The weather is used to reflect Johanna's and the Captain's moods, emotions, and relationship. In the beginning, it rains a lot. The two main characters' feelings are often those of sadness and storminess, but the longer they travel together, the warmer the days, and less rain falls.

1. "They are different when they come back." (Chapter 1, Page 10)

   Britt Johnson warns the Captain (and, vicariously, the reader) about the state-of-mind of returned captives and the difficulties in reintegrating them back into their old lives, and into European-American society. It introduces the topic of those caught between two very different worlds/cultures.

2. "It was in fact an excursion wagon painted a dark and glossy green and in gold letters on the sides it said *Curative Waters East Mineral Springs Texas* and he had no idea how the wagon had come all the way from near Houston to the little town on the Red River. The wagon surely had a story all to itself that would now remain forever unknown, untold." (Chapter 2, Page 14)

   The narrator places into the mind of the reader the idea of the transitory nature of life, its circular motion, and the importance of the present, an idea contrasting with the theme of memory and its importance. Though the wagon was previously used for something entirely different than the purposes for which the Captain has in mind for it, the metaphorical worth of its previous use—a vehicle for healing—remains intact.

3. "Then at last he was doing what he loved: carrying information by hand along through the Southern wilderness; messages, orders, maps, reports [...] He always recalled those two years with a kind of wonder. As when one is granted the life and the task for which one was meant." (Chapter 3, Pages 23-24)

The Captain knew from an early age just how much he loved and cherished the power of news and the written word, so much so that despite war and hardship, his raison d'être never waned. Further, he believes that by sharing news with others, he can make rural Texas society a better place.

4. "There is a repeat mechanism in the human mind that operates independently of will. The memory brought with it the vacuity of loss, irremediable loss, and so he told himself he would not indulge himself in memory but it could not be helped." (Chapter 3, Page 25)

   Memory is a strong theme throughout the novel. The problems and pain that arise from what one can and does remember is quickly introduced, especially the fact that memory is not something than can be controlled, willed. Both the Captain and Johanna struggle with thoughts from their pasts.

5. "If people had true knowledge of the world perhaps they would not take up arms and so perhaps he could be an aggregator of information from distant places and then the world would be a more peaceful place. He had been perfectly serious. That illusion had lasted from age forty-nine to age sixty-five." (Chapter 3, Page 29)

   Not only does this quote illustrate the Captain's love of news, but also his sense of idealism. Furthermore, it raises the question as to just what happened at the age of 65, a relatively late period in one's life, to have changed his belief in the healing power of the news. This question remains unanswered in the novel.

6. "Then the listeners would for a small space of time drift away into a healing place like curative waters." (Chapter 3, Page 30)

This quote ties in with the previous quote by reinforcing the fact that perhaps the news cannot end war permanently, but it can, nevertheless, halt feelings of anger and animosity for a space of time, and provide distraction and relief for the listeners.

7. "More than ever knowing in his fragile bones that it was the duty of men who aspired to the condition of humanity to protect children and kill for them if necessary." (Chapter 4, Page 38)

Long before the Captain even meets Almay, his philosophy regarding violence and protection is established. The quote illustrates the Captain's understanding of justice, one that goes a step above the law. It combines the toughness of frontier justice and self-preservation with that of the proper behavior of a civilized gentleman. It also foreshadows an upcoming confrontation wherein the Captain will have to revert to violence in order to protect Johanna.

8. "Then he sat on his own side of the wagon and saw her struggling with the fork, the knife, the stupidity of it, the unknown reasons that human beings would approach food in this manner, reasons incomprehensible, inexplicable, for which they had no common language." (Chapter 8, Page 76)

In this passage, we see the commonly-accepted made foreign via Johanna's inability to use an eating utensil. In doing so, the author shows the blending of cultures on the Texas plains: what is a given for one culture is an abnormality for another. Furthermore, it illustrates the Captain's ability to see beyond his own values and mores and sympathize with Johanna, something that is crucial for her survival in transitioning back in to European-American society.

9. "For a moment he was completely at a loss as to why he had agreed to take her to Castroville. For Britt. A freed black man. That's why." (Chapter 9, Page 86)

   The results of the Civil War and the outlawing of slavery are never directly addressed in the novel, but these topics nevertheless pop up in the background in multiple chapters. The exact relation between Britt and the Captain also remains unclear, but there are subtle hints that there is perhaps a sort of desire to make up for past, slavery-centered transgressions on the part of white Americans, and that the Captain is fully on board with the idea of integrating former slaves into American society.

10. "Someone called, Why are you not reading from Governor Davis' state journal? The Captain folded his newspapers. He said, Sir, you know very well why. He leaned forward over the podium. His white hair shone, his gold-rim glasses winked in the bull's-eye lantern beam. He was the image of elderly wisdom and reason. Because there would be a fistfight here within moments, if not shooting. Men have lost the ability to discuss any political event in Texas in a reasonable manner. There is no debate, only force. In point of fact, regard the soldiers beyond the door." (Chapter 10, Page 90)

    Despite his love for the news, the Captain also recognizes the negative aspect of the power of the

*written word, namely for it to be used to manipulate
and indoctrinate others with propaganda. Furthermore,
it illustrates the weaknesses in human beings in general
to be able to accept differing opinions of others. This
quote also highlights the political difficulties of
Southern Reconstruction following the Civil War.*

11. "Human aggression and depravity still managed to
    astonish him. He had been caught by surprise."
    (Chapter 11, Page 104)

    *People's evil towards others knows no bounds, an
    aphorism reinforced by this quote from the Captain. He
    is a man who has been in war and seen men die. He is
    not new to violence and depravity, and yet he still
    hasn't seen or read everything. This places in the
    reader's mind that perhaps there are other troubles
    ahead for him and Johanna that he cannot foresee.*

12. "Some people were born unsupplied with a human
    conscience and those people needed killing." (Chapter
    12, Page 110)

    *This quote illustrates the Captain's stance on justice.
    While he's haunted by memories of men dying during
    wars the Captain fought in, those men had a code of
    honor, and the Captain perceived them as decent
    people. This in stark contrast to someone like Almay,
    whom this quote references. Almay, as the leader of a
    child sex trafficking ring, is without any sort of moral
    code, and, in the Captain's eyes, the only proper end
    for such an individual is to be killed.*

13. "Maybe life is just carrying news. Surviving to carry
    the news. Maybe we have just one message, and it is
    delivered to us when we are born and we are never sure

what it says; it may have nothing to do with us personally but it must be carried by hand through a life, all the way, and at the end handed over, sealed." (Chapter 13, Page 120)

The Captain was a messenger while he was solider fighting in the War of 1812. From an early age, he knew the importance of information, but for the Captain, the importance of being a messenger goes beyond this life; it extends beyond the realm of the physical, earthly world. Being a messenger carries with it something metaphysical.

14. "The fool sat there and did that all day long and probably considered himself an expert on the English language because it spilled out of his mouth like water from an undershot brain and he didn't even have to think about it." (Chapter 14, Page 136)

The difficulty in communicating with people who speak different languages and the clash that comes about when people do not realize the intricacies of language, assuming that the language they speak is the one everyone should speak, is highlighted by the mill owner in Durand. Furthermore, the mill owner displays the discrepancies in language ability as a result of education.

15. "He was trying to care for a semi-savage girl child and fend off criminals who would kidnap her for the most dreadful purposes and at the same time make enough money in the only way he knew how so they might eat and travel and on top of that evade the brutal political clashes of Texans. A tall order." (Chapter 14, Page 136)

Here, we're offered all of the various adversities the Captain will face by agreeing to transport Johanna across Texas. The quote illustrates how the Captain must use both his intellect and his fighting skills in order to survive the trip.

16. "Well. But she must be corrected. She must have this forcefully impressed upon her. About modesty while bathing." (Chapter 14, Page 139)

The idea of cultural integration is a topic throughout the novel as the Captain gently instructs Johanna on European-American society. The Captain's methods are kind and patient. He understands the difficulties, the fear, and frustration involved in being caught between two very different worlds. The woman in Durand is not the only one who believes in forceful instruction, a topic that is revisited in the final chapters, when Johanna is delivered to her aunt and uncle. Further, the quote shows that while the Captain is accepting of cultures intersecting and blending, many on the Texas plains were not.

17. "He would have liked to kiss her on the cheek but he had no idea if the Kiowas kissed one another or if so, did grandfathers kiss granddaughters. You never knew. Cultures were mine fields." (Chapter 14, Page 140)

This illustrates the amazing understanding and caution that the Captain uses in dealing with Johanna. It illustrates how aware of the situation he is and how non-judgmental he can be in regard to Kiowa culture. It also provides a further example of just how difficult the interactions between peoples of different cultures can be.

18. "Captain Kidd said, It has been said by authorities that the law should apply the same to the king and to the peasant both, it should be written out and placed in the city square for all to see, it should be written simply and in the language of the common people, lest the people grow weary of their burdens. The young man tipped his head toward the Captain with an odd look on his face. It was a kind of longing, a kind of hope. Who said that? Hammurabi." (Chapter 15, Page 147)

The Captain is a learned, well-informed, and well-read man. Law and justice arise as topics in several places in the novel, and in a time of vast lawlessness caused by the insecurity of the frontier and Reconstruction, the Captain evokes the judicial philosophy of Hammurabi Code, one of the earliest written legal documents (18th century BC).

19. "Loss of reputation and the regard of our fellow persons is in any society, from Iceland to East Indies, a terrible blow to the spirit. It is worse than being penniless and more cutting than the blades of enemies." (Chapter 15, Page 150)

This quote illustrates the recurrent motif of a person needing to have a code of honor. The Captain lives by a very strict code of honor to which he refers when having to make certain moral decisions. His reputation is very important to him. These are core characteristics of his.

20. "I see. The Captain was silent a moment, puzzling over the Horrell brothers, people whose minds were lost in such delusions, such avid desire for worldly fame." (Chapter 16, Page 162)

The Horrell brothers desire to be known for their exploits, which involve hunting down and killing Mexicans; they ask the Captain if they are mentioned in the newspapers he has bought. This quote points out a contradictory element in the Captain's belief system. The reading of the news, of passing along story-worthy deeds, is the very thing that fuels fame. The more people read and know of another's exploits, the more famous that person becomes (or infamous). Thus, the Captain is at least potentially a catalyst for the very thing he is criticizing.

21. "Raiding parties of young men had their own laws and their own universe in which the niceties of civilized warfare did not count and an old man and a young girl were fair game to them, for in the Indian Wars there were no civilians." (Chapter 18, Page 172)

    This illustrates the brutality of the Indian Wars and guerrilla warfare in general, juxtaposing it with what is known as "civilized" warfare—the idea of two armies meeting on an open battlefield, blazing away at well-formed lines of musketmen, and conforming to a specific, mostly unwritten code of conduct. The Civil War and the late 19th-century was a transition period between the old methods of warfare to modern warfare.

22. "He saw her bright, fierce face break into laughter when the crowd laughed. It was good. Laughter is good for the soul and all your interior works." (Chapter 18, Page 176)

    Johanna has not had an easy time of things. She has lost her parents, been kidnapped, been raised by a culture vastly different than her own, and then been brought back to a culture she no longer knows, to be taken care of by strangers. And yet in spite of hardship, she can still find ways to be positive, to laugh, and enjoy life. Laughter's healing effects go hand in hand with the "curative waters" motif and the idea of healing from past suffering.

23. "The greatest pride of the Kiowa was to do without, to make use of anything at hand; they were almost vain of their ability to go without water, food, shelter. Life was not safe and nothing could make it so, neither fashionable dresses nor bank accounts. The baseline of human life was courage." (Chapter 22, Page 201)

The Kiowa are used as a counterbalance for Anglo-American culture and society, as something to measure itself against, to compare itself to, and to judge itself. It highlights the Spartan lifestyle of not only the Kiowa but also the Plains Indians in general. The Captain seems to harbor a good amount of respect for the Kiowa, while at the same time understanding himself as different than them and being wary of them.

24. "Johanna turned and put her arms around the Captain's neck. We will come to visit often, she said. You are my cuuative watah [curative waters]. Then she began to sob." (Chapter 22, Page 208)

This quote is from the very end of the book; Johanna has grown up and is married, and the Captain is quite old. Johanna, through her sobs, shows how thankful she is for the Captain protecting her and taking her away from her aunt and uncle. She now has a family of her own, and is happy.

25. "In his will the Captain asked to be buried with his runner's badge. He had kept it since 1814. He said he

had a message to deliver, contents unknown." (Chapter 22, Page 209)

The Captain has spent his life in the service of delivering both items and people to others. Here, as he departs from the world, he asks to be buried with his runner's badge, that item that most fully symbolizes his place in the world.

ESSAY TOPICS

1. In what way(s) does Captain Kidd's work as a newspaper reader affect both himself and those to whom he reads?

2. Why does Captain Kidd accept the difficult task of taking Johanna to her aunt and uncle, and what keeps him motivated while he is en route?

3. Why does Johanna identify most with her Kiowa family? What allows her to reintegrate into European-American society?

4. What characteristics bring Johanna and the Captain together? What is it about him that causes her to trust him?

5. What is it that most worries the Captain about what fate awaits Johanna, after she's returned to her relatives? What has he heard about other returned captives?

6. Doris Dillon says that Johanna is "carried away on the flood of the world," that she is "not real and not not-real," that she "has been through two creations" (56). Is Doris correct in her description of Johanna's state?

7. In what ways does language function in the novel? Is any single language treated as being more important or better than another?

8. What different forms of law are portrayed in the novel? What does this tell the reader about Texas during this time period?

9. The adjective "American" is never used to describe someone in the novel. Why is this? What effect does this have on the identities of the characters?

10. What are the pros and cons of the news in the novel? How is news both something positive and negative for the communities the Captain passes through?

Made in the USA
Monee, IL
18 September 2019